Smell of the Rain
Voices of the Stars

written by NORIHISA AKAZA
illustrated by YOSHIHARU SUZUKI
translated by EIJI SEKINE

HARCOURT BRACE & COMPANY

Orlando   Atlanta   Austin   Boston   San Francisco   Chicago   Dallas   New York
Toronto   London

This edition is published by special arrangement with Japan Foreign-Rights Centre, on behalf of Komine Shoten Publishing Company Ltd., Tokyo, Japan.

English translation copyright © 1994 by Harcourt Brace & Company

Grateful acknowledgment is made to Japan Foreign-Rights Centre, on behalf of Komine Shoten Publishing Company Ltd., Tokyo, Japan, for permission to reprint *Smell of the Rain, Voices of the Stars* by Norihisa Akaza, illustrated by Yoshiharu Suzuki. Copyright © 1987 by Norihisa Akaza and Yoshiharu Suzuki. Originally published in Japan under the title *Ame No Nioi Hoshi No Koe*.

Printed in the United States of America

ISBN 0-15-302204-3

4 5 6 7 8 9 10   011   97 96 95

Smell of the Rain
Voices of the Stars

written by NORIHISA AKAZA

illustrated by YOSHIHARU SUZUKI

translated by EIJI SEKINE

"A Pouring Rain"

As rain began to fall,
I could smell the soil—
The smell of the earth
In the pouring rain.

This poem was written by Mashio, a fourth grader, blind from his birth. He tells of a sudden evening shower meeting the dry soil of the school ground.

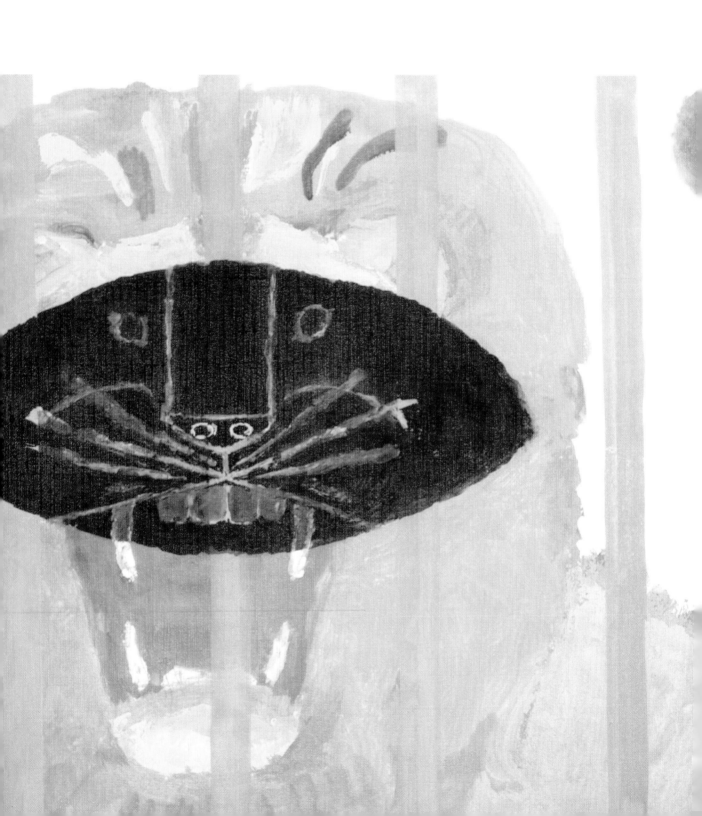

A Lion

The blind children played happily with a puppy. Then they made puppies with modeling clay. Puppies and more puppies tumbled from each child's hands!

The children also made clay cats and bunnies after they had played with real ones. And when they created a horse, they remembered how it felt when they sat on the back of a real horse.

Once, the children went to the zoo, where they were impressed by the tremendous roar of a lion. Later, when they worked on clay lions, the first thing everyone made was a huge, open mouth full of sharp teeth.

Wind

*When the children felt
the wind, it appeared to them
as shapes on the screen behind
their unseeing eyes.*

"Here comes a round wind."
"Let's chase the round wind."
"This is a long, skinny wind."
"Let's catch the skinny one."

*As they chased and were
chased by the wind, the blind
children became good friends
with it.*

A Gaze

Miiko once said to me, "Gaze is a word heard often, isn't it?"

"What? Gaze?"

"Yes. You know, someone might say that two people gaze at each other."

"I see. Well, it means that one's eyes meet another person's eyes."

"But what exactly happens when one person's eyes meet with another's?"

Since I had never seriously thought about this familiar expression, I did not know how to answer Miiko.

Then, pressing one of her blind eyes with her index finger, Miiko gently touched my eye with her other index finger. I felt indeed as if she "gazed" into my eyes.

Touching a Statue of Buddha

There are things that you cannot understand without touching them; but there are also things that you cannot understand even after touching them. If touching helps you understand things a little better, surely you should try to touch as many things as you can. Yet, there are many things that you are not allowed to touch.

One day our school received special permission from a temple for our children to touch a real statue of Buddha. Miiko softly touched the statue with both hands, whispering to herself, "…round, very round, and smooth, and heartwarming …"

Touched for the first time by so many children's hands, the Buddha statue looked ticklish, and it seemed as if his eyes smiled into the unseeing eyes of the children.

Sports

To play volleyball, the blind children roll a ball on the ground, back and forth under the volleyball net.

For baseball, they roll a soccer ball. In order for a runner not to bump against defensive players, the children use a set of defensive bases, in addition to the regular offensive bases.

To play table tennis, they hit the ball with their rackets so that it goes under the net.

When a game day is coming, all the children practice hard. By listening to the rolling sound of a ball, they can judge when and where to hit it or catch it. In their imagination, of course, the balls are flying high in the air!

A School Picture

"Let's have our picture taken together." These words of mine really excited the children.

When we received our school picture, each child told me correctly where he or she was to be found in the photo. One said, "I'm the second person from the right." Then another said, "I am in the middle of the second row."

"What do I look like in this photo?" asked Miiko.

How should I answer her? Finally I replied, "Well, let me see. I think you… you look just like you!"

Hearing this, Miiko nodded deeply, her dimples disappearing behind her serious look.

A Snow-Covered Mountain Pass

On the last day of the winter break, Akio returned to the school for the blind, located in town. It was a sunny day, and his younger brother held his hand as they crossed a snow-covered mountain pass. As they walked, their straw boots made squeaky noises. They felt each other's palms begin to sweat.

At the top of the mountain, they stopped for a short rest. As he was wiping snow off his little brother's boots, Akio said, "I hear a siskin chirping. Now a chickadee has just sung."

His brother replied, "Oh yes, I saw the chickadee."

Their eyes, with and without sight, stared at each other.

Then Akio's little brother found rabbit tracks in the snow. He looked long at the shining tracks, wishing he could describe them to Akio.

A Flower Pot

" ... I was squatting, holding a flower pot upside down. I poked my finger through the little hole in the bottom of the pot. The soil dropped on the ground, making a rather heavy sound. I wanted to know what this mass of soil felt like. I touched it and realized that it was shaped like a pot and was filled with a lot of plant roots. After throwing the soil away, I took the pot to the well and washed it. While I was cleaning it thoroughly with all my fingers, it started to make a sound, saying shoo-shoo. I then touched my ear to the surface of the pot: I heard it sing various songs, while water dripped into my ear."

Keizo wrote this essay when he was a fifth grader. When the dry flower pot suddenly absorbed water, it made all kinds of faint noises. Keizo put his cheek to the pot and exclaimed happily, "I hear songs. The flower pot is singing!"

A Visit to a Garden of Roses

One day we went to see roses. Those with no sight can easily tell differences between roses by their smell.

"This flower smells like a kitten's back."

"This smells like a knitted sweater."

"Smell this one. Its smell reminds me of the sound of a flute."

"This one's smell is just like that of an apple core."

"This smells like a lemon."

"And this like a cream puff!"

Smelling different roses one by one, they kept trying to describe each one's scent. After a while, I noticed that everybody had started to refer to something to eat. All the children laughed when I mentioned this!

A Field Trip

The children were going on a field trip. Each one held a white cane with one hand and the hand of his or her partner with the other.

When the children go along a road they know well, they walk proudly, chatting loudly to one another. When a road is new to them, they walk as if their whole bodies have turned into a big, careful ear. They can tell when they come to an intersection, because the wind changes its direction there. They can also judge where they are by the sounds of the crowd and the traffic, and the voices of different people.

They walked along a street paved with asphalt, then a gravel road, and then a road scattered with weeds. Through the feelings that came from their feet, the children pictured different scenes as they passed by.

At the River Beach

The blind children love to come to a river beach. They run along the rocky beach and turn their faces toward the wide flow of water.

Each one picks up a small rock and throws it toward the water with all his or her force. The size of the rock, the depth of the water, and the speed of the water flow determine the sound that each rock makes as it drops into the water. The children listen carefully to each throw of a rock and shout together when they hear the rock fall into the water. In their imagination, they picture the ripples expanding along the surface of the water.

Radio and Television

"Since they cannot see, they must like radio better than TV." Many people assume this, but the truth seems to be just the opposite!

"On the radio news, I don't hear the sound made by an anchor person when he or she turns the page of the manuscript," said one of our students. If you stop to think of it, you realize that television lets such sounds transmit freely. Our children like to hear those kinds of sounds.

"Sports announcers on the radio talk too much," said another student. It's true that on TV the screen sometimes lets pictures run with no words. But many children who are blind enjoy being able to imagine scenes in silence.

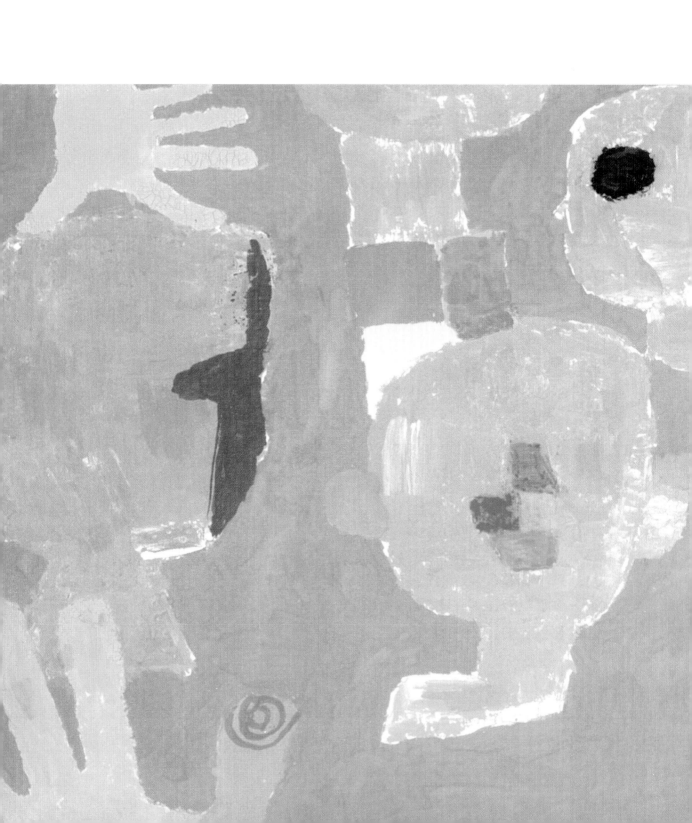

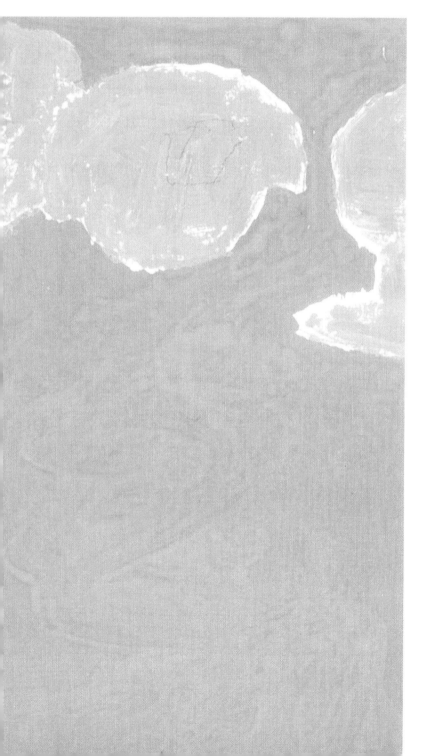

Modeling Clay

Since they wash their faces every morning, the blind children know what their faces look like. When I ask them to create portraits of themselves in clay, they start to work eagerly. The faces they model differ from one another, but one thing they have in common is the largeness of the eye sockets. Some children attach big eyeballs to the face, and some leave the eyes as deep hollows. In both cases, their fingers express their keen desire to be able to see the world.

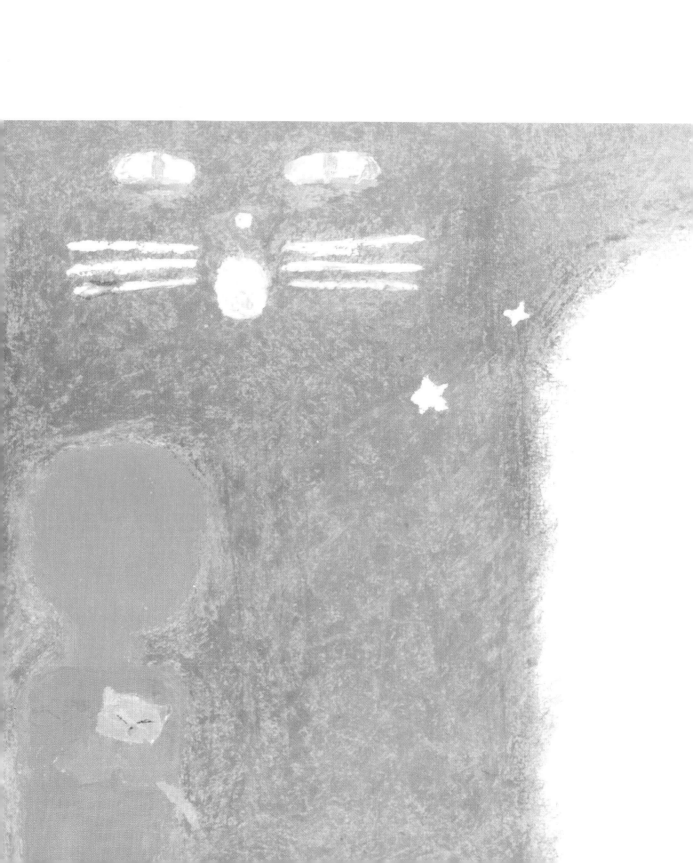

"Stars"

They say the stars are twinkling.
I have not seen their light.
But I feel their sharp twinkle is
Like a cat's cry at night.

This is a poem written by Akio when he was in the fourth grade. Akio cannot see how wide the sky is or how brightly the stars shine. However, he imagines the "twinkle" he has heard about by identifying it with the sharp cry of a cat, a sound he enjoys.

Thanks to Akio's imagination, we can all hear the cry of the cat echo into the depths of the night sky.

POSTSCRIPT

Children who are blind write their poems and essays by using Braille. Letters in Braille are patterns of dots raised on the surface of the paper. They look like the eggs of a moth. By touching these dot patterns with the tips of their fingers, blind people can read.

The words of any book can be set in Braille, but not the pictures the book may contain. Since the number of books published in Braille is so limited, we need to work on making more books available in Braille.

A book in Braille is bulky. When a regular children's book is set in Braille, the pages turn out as big as magazine pages, and the "book" is really two or three volumes, each about seven centimeters thick. Some are even thicker. However, skilled readers of Braille read as fast as, or even faster than, readers of regular print.

I worked at a school for the blind in Gifu Prefecture for seventeen years (from 1954 through 1971). My blind students taught me about many things that I did not notice or even think about before I started working with them.

I wrote this book in the hope that it would help sighted people develop an understanding of the richness of the blind person's world. The book consists of selected episodes that I still see today in my dreams.

[Additional information on the names referred to in the text]

Mashio: Tooyama Mashio ("A Pouring Rain," July 1954)

Akio: Nakai Akio ("Stars," July 1954)

Keizo: Yamada Keizo ("A Flower Pot," September 1959)

Miiko: a girl created in my imagination